I0102022

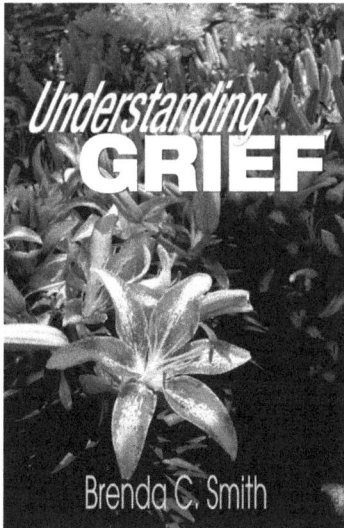

*Understanding*
GRIEF

Brenda C. Smith

# *Understanding* GRIEF

## Brenda C. Smith

inCahoots LITERARY
Oklahoma City

© Brenda C. Smith 2019. All rights reserved.

No part of this book may be reproduced in any form or by any means without permission in writing from the publisher, except for the inclusion of brief quotations in a review.

**irCahoots**
**LITERARY**

Published by InCahoots Literary
a division of InCahoots Film Entertainment LLC
Oklahoma City

www.incahootsliterary.com
www.incahootsfilmentertainment.com

Book design and cover photography by Michael Allen of InCahoots Literary

Back cover self-photograph by Brenda C. Smith

ISBN 978-1-7341937-0-1

# Dedication

This book is dedicated to all the loved ones I had to grieve for and whose lives have left an indelible imprint on my heart forever. To the ones who are resting in the family plot: Bertha (Mama), James (Brother), Michael (Brother), Larry (Brother). To my husband, Michael, in the "Field of Honor" in Pegram, Tennessee. To Gloria and Carolyn (sisters). All of you will be remembered, forever.

Your lives will be recalled at our family gatherings at Thanksgiving and Christmas, each birthday, and each anniversary of your deaths. You will always be spoken of with love and adoration, because the love we shared shall live on eternally. I thank God for the balm he has applied to promote in the healing of this mourning journey.

*"For I am convinced that neither death nor life, neither angels nor demons, neither the present nor the future, nor any powers,* [39] *neither height nor depth, nor anything else in all creation, will be able to separate us from the love of God that is in Christ Jesus our Lord."* – Romans 8:38-39.

Thank you for all you have given me to keep me moving forward in my life. All the life lessons, laughter, joy, and love are mine forever. God planned this family for me and God has given me great reminders of you all. *"So now faith, hope, and love abide, these three; but the greatest of these is love."* – I Corinithians 13:13 (The Love Chapter).

OUR FAMILY: Circle of Strength, founded on faith, joined in LOVE, kept by God.

# Contents

# Acknowledgements

I would like to acknowledge the presence of the Holy Spirit who is my Comforter and my Strength. For without His presence I would not be able to stand and do the things God has called me to do in this life. I am forever grateful for your love, comfort, and presence being in my healing in Jesus name.

My children have shown great strength throughout my mourning journey: Quinton, Quinesha, and Quandré have been here for me in ways I cannot explain. Their constant attention to my needs and my well-being have been so inspiring. Although they were grieving, they always took time to check in on me. And for this I will forever be grateful.

To a wonderful man who's light shineth one day upon my path. The one who God had to have sent because my heart was not in a place to receive the love he was so ready to give. To Melvin Pope, the guiding light and constant reassuring voice who convinced me that life could once again be filled with hope and love.

To all the people who prayed for me. You never forgot to ask about me, send me encouragement, calls, text messages, or a visit. These beautiful, loving, and dedicated people of the Household of Faith of the Green Street Church of God. I love you! You never forgot me, and I am grateful.

FAMILY IS EVERYTHING:

To Lina Fitzgerald, my sister, for her strength and determination to carry on with her life. Her quiet example of love showed me a new path.

To Cheryl Steele, my sister, for her care and concern. Your smile meant everything to me.

To Katherine Shelton, my sister, how you showed me how to pull back up from adversity. That life may knock you down, but you must "rise again."

To Robert Covington, my brother, who's voice was one of assurance and love. His prayers and guidance helped me along this path. I am forever grateful in how you came and stood with me throughout each  funeral, and your strength alone was indeed my strength.

WE ARE FAMILY: The Steele Family. The Covington Family. The McCullough Family. The Harrison Family. The Smith Family. You are all too numerous to name individually, but I love you all and thank you for all you did for me and my family.

# Introduction

How Did I Get Here? I suppose you are wondering why I would consider writing a self-help book for people who are grieving? I suppose you are wondering why it is of such interest to me?

I have experienced the loss of many of my loved ones. For me it started in March, 2010, when I was devastated by the loss of Michael, my husband. Michael and I had been married at that time for thirty years. We had been college sweethearts, and I had gone with him as he served in the United States Air Force. We served together as husband and wife, and we were just learning all the wonders of the "married life." Michael and I had a strong and very loving three years, just the two of us, while in Cheyenne, Wyoming. We saw the birth of our firstborn son while there. We learned and carried with us those long days of talking and planning our lives and living for the time we would separate from the Armed Services and start our lives together. God blessed us with three children and after Michael's death, a grandson.

Death isn't something most people sit down and discuss. We are so busy living our lives that death is not on our minds nor a part of our daily vocabulary. That is why when it happens it is such a shock to you! It happened and then I was left with the task of, "How Do I Carry On?" Just how do I live from day to day knowing that the one I had spent so much of my life with is never going to be here, again. How do you teach your children how to live again? I have my focus because I had my three children and I knew they needed me. I had no idea how to move past all that hurt and pain.

In my group of close friends, they understood only to a certain degree of what I was feeling. None of my close friends had lost a husband. I had to figure out where to go and who to talk to in this grieving process. Because I am a Christian and a child of God, I immediately went to the Bible for instructions on how to LIVE, again. Scripture tells us that death is just a part of life. "And as it is appointed unto men once to die, but after this the judgment" (Hebrews 9:27). And it was a blessing to those who had died. Then I heard a voice from heaven say, "Write this: Blessed are the dead who die in the Lord from now on." "Yes," says the Spirit, "they will rest from their labor, for their deeds will follow them" (Revelation 14:13).

Lord, I need a blessing from you in order to continue to live my life. This is where I was when death first happened. I was lost, confused, hurting, in pain, crying, and in need of healing. So, as in most cases, when I am in need; I sought help.

I pray these pages in this book will strengthen you and help you to seek healing for the pain that you are in. Help is there, and you do not have to suffer, nor struggle alone.

Brenda C. Smith

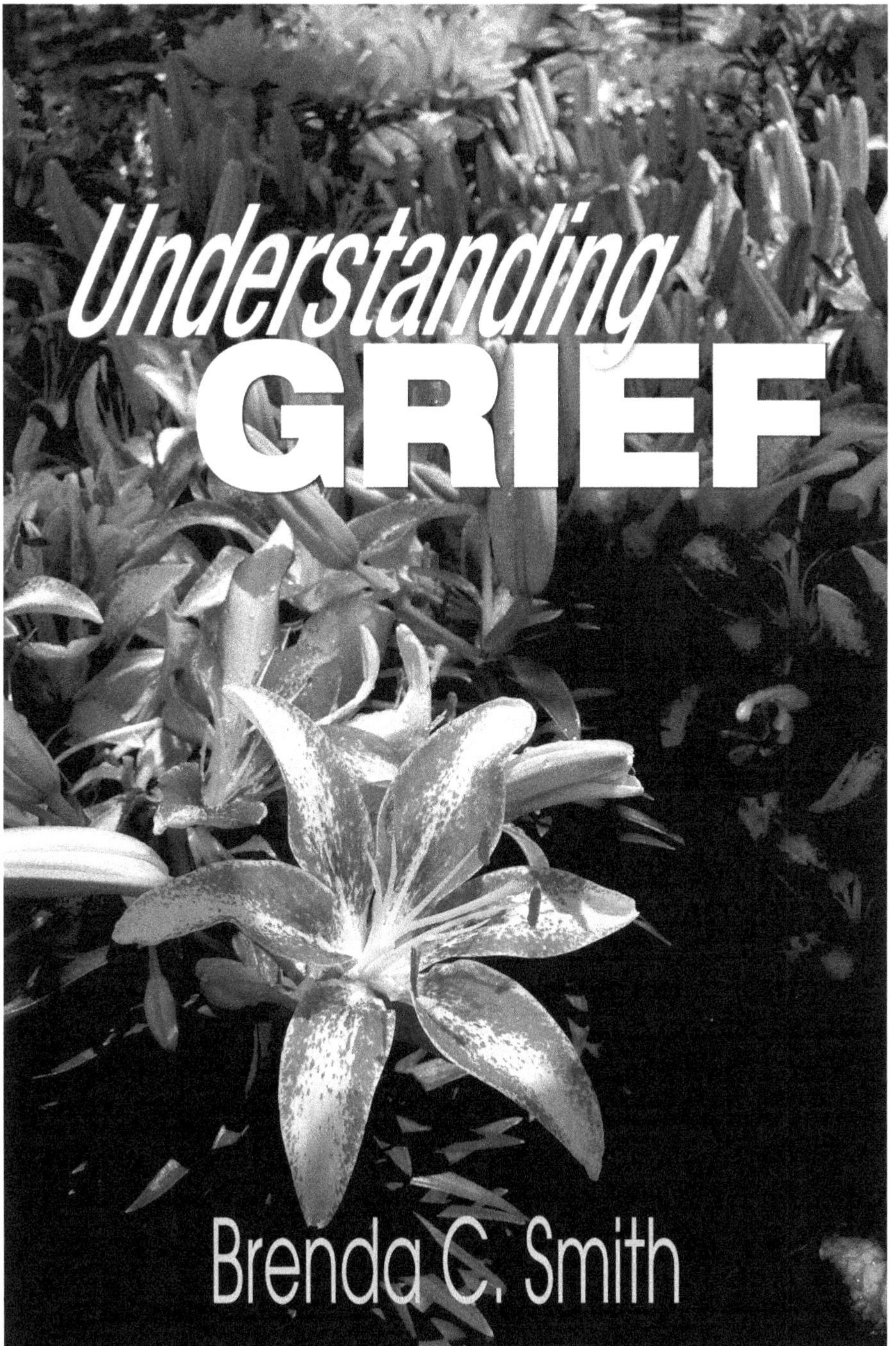
Understanding
GRIEF
Brenda C. Smith

An important part of overcoming grief is expressing it to God. *"I write these things to you who believe in the name of the Son of God so that you may know that you have eternal life."* (I John 5:12)

# The Five Stages of Grief

Grieving is a "normal" process of life. It is normal and natural for you to grieve the loss of your loved ones, your long term relationships, and careers. People have lost careers they have built for over thirty to forty years. When they are gone, there is a natural response to this as a loss, and it needs to be mourned over and then you move on.

The five stages of grief are "normal" processes. They may happen in any order and may include additional emotions.

## Denial

The first emotion is a defense mechanism that protects against the emotional shock or pain of death.

## Anger

This intense emotion is projected onto others.
It may be first to the doctor who you felt may not have done all he/she could to save your loved one's life.

## Bargaining

The feelings of helplessness are accompanied by regrets.
Feelings that may arise are "We should have noticed the signs earlier." We may make promises to God in this stage.
"I promise never to lie if my loved one survives this illness."

## Depression

Feelings of loss, sadness and regret take hold.

# Acceptance
In this stage, terminally ill patients or their loved ones
come to terms with the inevitable. During the
acceptance stage, people allow themselves
to feel their grief and emotions fully.

The death of your loved one might inspire you to evaluate your
own feelings of mortality. Throughout each stage, a common
thread of hope emerges: As long as there is life, there is hope. As
long as there is hope, there is life.

Please keep in mind that everyone grieves differently. Some people
will wear their emotions on their sleeve and be outwardly emotional. Others will experience their grief more internally and may
not cry. You should not judge how a person experiences their grief,
as each person will experience it differently.

# The Five Stages of Grief – Expanded

**Denial**

Denial is the stage that can initially help you survive the loss. You might think life makes no sense, has no meaning, and is too overwhelming. You start to deny the news and, in effect, go numb. It's common in this stage to wonder how life will go on in this different state – you are in a state of shock because life as you once knew it, has changed in an instant. If you were diagnosed with a deadly disease, you might believe the news is incorrect – a mistake must have occurred somewhere in the lab–they mixed up your blood work with someone else. If you receive news on the death of a loved one, perhaps you cling to a false hope that they identified the wrong person. In the denial stage, you are not living in 'actual reality,' rather, you are living in a 'preferable' reality. Interestingly, it is denial and shock that help you cope and survive the grief event. Denial aids in pacing your feelings of grief. Instead of becoming completely overwhelmed with grief, we deny it, do not accept it, and stagger its full impact on us at one time. Think of it as your body's natural defense mechanism saying "hey, there's only so much I can handle at once." Once the denial and shock starts to fade, the start of the healing process begins. At this point, those feelings that you were once suppressing are coming to the surface.

**Anger**

Once you start to live in 'actual' reality again and not in 'preferable' reality, anger might start to set in. This is a common stage to think "why me?" and "life's not fair!" You might look to blame others for the cause of your grief and also may redirect your anger to close friends and family. You find it incomprehensible of how something like this could happen to you. If you are strong in faith, you might start to question your belief in God. "Where is God? Why didn't he protect me?"

Researchers and mental health professionals agree that this anger is a necessary stage of grief. And encourage the anger. It's important to truly feel the anger. It's thought that even though you might seem like you are in an endless cycle of anger, it will dissipate – and the more you truly feel the anger, the more quickly it will dissipate, and the more quickly you will heal. It is not healthy to suppress your feelings of anger – it is a natural response – and perhaps, arguably, a necessary one. In every day life, we are normally told to control our anger toward situations and toward others.

When you experience a grief event, you might feel disconnected from reality – that you have no grounding anymore. Your life has shattered and there's nothing solid to hold onto. Think of anger as a strength to bind you to reality. You might feel deserted or abandoned during a grief event. That no one is there. You are alone in this world. The direction of anger toward something or somebody is what might bridge you back to reality and connect you to people again. It is a "thing." It's something to grasp onto – a natural step in healing.

**Bargaining**

When something bad happens, have you ever caught yourself making a deal with God? "Please God, if you heal my husband, I will strive to be the best wife I can ever be – and never complain again." This is bargaining. In a way, this stage is false hope. You might falsely make yourself believe that you can avoid the grief through a type of negotiation. If you change this, I'll change that. You are so desperate to get your life back to how it was before the grief event, you are willing to make a major life change in an attempt toward normality. Guilt is a common wing man of bargaining. This is when you endure the endless "what if" statements. What if I had left the house 5 minutes sooner – the accident would have never happened. What if I encouraged him to go to the doctor six months ago like I first thought – the cancer could have been found sooner and he could have been saved.

## Depression

Depression is a commonly accepted form of grief. In fact, most people associate depression immediately with grief – as it is a "present" emotion. It represents the emptiness we feel when we are living in reality and realize the person or situation is gone or over. In this stage, you might withdraw from life, feel numb, live in a fog, and not want to get out of bed. The world might seem too much and too overwhelming for you to face. You don't want to be around others, don't feel like talking, and experience feelings of hopelessness. You might even experience suicidal thoughts – thinking "what's the point of going on?"

## Acceptance

The last stage of grief identified by Kübler-Ross is acceptance. Not in the sense that "it's okay my husband died" rather, "my husband died, but I'm going to be okay." In this stage, your emotions may begin to stabilize. You re-enter reality. You come to terms with the fact that the "new" reality is that your partner is never coming back – or that you are going to succumb to your illness and die soon – and you're okay with that. It's not a "good" thing – but it's something you can live with. It is definitely a time of adjustment and readjustment. There are good days, there are bad days, and then there are good days again. In this stage, it does not mean you'll never have another bad day – where you are uncontrollably sad. But, the good days tend to outnumber the bad days. In this stage, you may lift from your fog, you start to engage with friends again, and might even make new relationships as time goes on. You understand your loved one can never be replaced, but you move, grow, and evolve into your new reality.

# Symptoms of Grief

Your grief symptoms may present themselves physically, socially, or spiritually. Some of the most common symptoms of grief are presented below:

**Crying**
**Headaches**
**Difficulty Sleeping**
**Questioning the Purpose of Life**
**Questioning Your Spiritual Beliefs**
      (your belief in God)
**Feelings of Detachment**
**Isolation from Friends and Family**
**Abnormal Behavior**
**Worry**
**Anxiety**
**Frustration**
**Guilt**
**Fatigue**
**Anger**
**Loss of Appetite**
**Aches and Pains**
**Stress**

# Bereavement Symptoms

Bereavement is a normal reaction to loss in virtually every culture across the world. There are no set rules for how long "normal" bereavement lasts, as each person and each loss are very different. Therefore, bereavement tends not to be diagnosed unless it has gone on for a very significant period of time and significantly impacts the person's life. Getting over or past the loss of a loved one can be challenging for nearly everyone.

For some, the loss of a loved one is too much, causing them to enter into a clinical depression that may need further attention or treatment.

Bereavement is diagnosed when the focus of clinical attention is a reaction to the death or loss of a loved one. As part of their reaction to the loss, some grieving individuals have symptoms characteristic of a major depressive episode (e.g., feelings of sadness and associated symptoms such as insomnia, poor appetite, and weight loss).

The bereaved individual typically regards the depressed mood as normal, although the person may seek professional help for relief of associated symptoms such as insomnia. The duration and expression of a normal bereavement vary considerably among different cultural groups.

The diagnosis of major depressive disorder is not given unless the symptoms are still present two months after the loss.

The presence of certain symptoms that are not characteristic of a normal grief reaction may be helpful in differentiating bereavement from a major depressive episode.

These include:

1. Guilt about things other than actions taken or not taken by the survivor at the time of the death;

2. Thoughts of death other than the survivor feeling that he or she would be better off dead or should have died with the deceased person;

3. Morbid preoccupation with worthlessness;

4. Significant psychomotor retardation (e.g., it's hard to get moving, and what movements there are are slow);

5. Prolonged and serious functional impairment; and

6. Hallucinatory experiences other than thinking that he or she hears the voice of the deceased person or transiently sees the image of the deceased person.

# What You Might *Not* Expect
# With the Loss of a Loved One

You are going to feel all sort of emotions as you work through your mourning journey. You will be sad, you will at times feel hopeless, helpless, and it all depends on which loved one you have lost to death. These feelings and emotions are in the five stages of grief:

**Denial:** "No, it can't be."

**Anger:** "Who's responsible? How did this happen?"

**Bargaining:** "I would do anything to have them back."

**Depression:** "I can't go on."

**Acceptance:** "There was nothing I could have done."

But there are other emotions and feelings you may experience. Some of these even to me were difficult to admit.

**Stuck** – For the first few months, I often felt "stuck" when thinking about my husband and the future ahead. I could no longer make plans as I did in the past. His death was so sudden, that I did not have time to plan anything. I wasn't given an opportunity to talk to him about death or any plans he wanted for a funeral.

I felt detached from friends and co-workers as if I was at a standstill or even detached from the rest of the world and what was going on around me. I had to somehow put on a smile and push down my other feelings and learn how to cope, but it only kept me feeling stuck in my grief.

I understood how fragile life is in part of the *stuckness* I was feeling.

**Clinging** – I soon found myself feeling overprotective of the things they left behind. I was clinging to those items and not wanting to clean out their clothing, sell furniture, or part with those memories. It is not unusual to want to hold on to their items. Some people keep voicemail recordings so they can hear their loved one voices. Some people even keep rooms the same way they were when their loved one died. You cling to these things because in your mind that is all you have left of them.

It may be difficult to share any of these items with others, but part with them when you feel you are ready to do so. Other family members would like to have items to hold and keep close to their hearts, too.

**Relief** – Every once in a while, perhaps you have felt relief of a loved one passing. If you were a caregiver attending to a person's needs for months or years at a time, when they die, you may find yourself feeling thankful. This is not a reason for you to beat yourself up and start to feel guilty about what you are feeling. Relief means feeling of reassurance and relaxation following release from anxiety or distress. Your relief may be that they are "no longer suffering." You may find it difficult to share this emotion with others – for fear of being judged. When a person was terminally ill, and they have suffered for many years, and they couldn't be healed; you may feel relief that it is over for them.

**Stay True to Yourself** – Remember, grief is different for everyone. No one experiences the loss of a loved one, whether the relationship was positive or negative in the same way. Your journey through grief will be your own. Be sure you talk, write, or share your thoughts with others. This will help you move through the phases of grief more easily.

When I was writing this book, putting my thoughts to paper, the process has been more than therapeutic; it has also re-opened my creative door. I can share with you what I went through and facing each death was different. My hope is you open yourself up to healing and allow others to share with you their emotions and concerns. It is okay to pour your heart out to others, because many are in need of release and relief of these emotions.

Healing starts with You.

# Forty Things I Wish
# They Had Told Me About Grief

A list of some of the things I wished I had known about grief before it happened to me. If I had been taught how to react to some of the silly things people would say? If I had a response to give back to them when they said it. But no one said it, because most times no on wants to talk about death.

I wish someone had told me:

1. No matter how prepared you think you are for a death, you can never be fully prepared for the loss and the grief.

2. You can plan for death, but death does not always comply with our wishes or plans.

3. Stop avoiding and be present.

4. Dying is not like you see on TV or in the movies. It is not peaceful or prepared. You may not have a spiritual or meaningful moment. It's too real.

5. A hospital death is not always a bad death.

6. A home death/hospice death is not always a good death.

7. There will be pressure from others to move on, even minutes or hours after a death, and this can lead to regrets.

8. Death is not an emergency. There is always a time to step back and take a moment to say "goodbye."

9. Death and grief make people uncomfortable, so be prepared for awkward encounters.

10. You will plan the funeral while in a haze. If you aren't happy with the funeral you had, have another memorial service later.

11. When people offer support, take them up on it.

12. People will bring you food because they don't know what else to do. Don't feel bad throwing it away.

13. People will say stupid, hurtful things without even realizing it.

14. People will tell you things that aren't true about your grief.

15. Death brings out the best and the worst in families, so be prepared.

16. There is no such thing as closure.

17. There is no timeline for grieving. You can't rush it. You will grieve in some form, forever.

18. There will always be regrets. No matter how much time you had, you'll always want more.

19. Guilt is a normal part of grief.

20. Anger is normal part of grief.

21. The pain of a loss is a reflection of love, but you never regret loving as hard as you can.

22. Grief can make you question your faith.

23. Grief doesn't come in five neat stages. Grief is messy and confusing.

24. Grief makes you feel like you're going crazy.

25. Grief can make you question your life, your purpose, and your goals. And that isn't always a bad thing.

26. We all grieve differently, which can create strain and confusion between family members and friends.

27. However, badly you think it is going to hurt, it is going to be a million times worse.

28. You may find comfort in very unexpected places.

29. You should go somewhere to debrief after caregiving.

30. The last twenty-four hours of their lives will replay in your mind.

31. Trying to protect children from death and the emotions of grief isn't helpful.

32. It's sometimes necessary to seek out new ways to grieve on your own and find new guidance if the people who are supposed to be supportive simply haven't learned how.

33. You grieve your past, present, and future with that person.

34. Big life events and milestones will forever be bittersweet.

35. Grief triggers are everywhere. You will see things that remind you of your loved one all over the place, and it may lead to sudden outbursts of emotion.

36. You lose yourself, your identity, meaning, purpose, values, and your trust.

37. Holidays, anniversaries, and birthdays will be hard forever.

38. People will tell you what you should and shouldn't feel and how you should and shouldn't grieve. Ignore them.

39. The grief process is about not only mourning the loss, but getting to know yourself as a different person.

40. There is no normal when it comes to grieving.

# The One to Two Year Myth

Myth is a widely held but false belief or an idea.

When are you going to get over losing the loved one? Why is it taking so long to move on? Some have stated that it takes going through that first year. Others say, give it two years and things will start to turn around for the good. Living as we do in a culture having no tolerance for pain of any kind - especially the physical, psychological, social, and spiritual agony of grief – it's no wonder people who are grieving feel abnormal when they can't stop their pain.

"No! This can't be happening!" This is our initial reaction when confronted with devastating news, as we resist facing the awful truth. This phase of protest may be present for months (in extreme, complicated cases, for years), particularly if the death was sudden, and especially if the bereaved did not see the person's body after they died. People in protest may try to avoid any evidence that contributes to acknowledging the painful reality of this loss.

Among those whose mourning rituals permit viewing of the deceased, such viewing is an important component of the work of grief, as it confirms the fact that the person has, in fact, died. And yet, more and more families are opting for direct cremation with no viewing. If the bereaved were not present when the person died and then refuse or decline to see the deceased prior to cremation or burial, complicated or protracted bereavement may result. Many will report fantasies that their loved ones are not really dead; that it was a big mistake.

Once the psyche acknowledges the sad reality that a loved one has died, profound despair may follow, along with symptoms that constitute a major or clinical depression. While the symptoms may appear identical, the treatment of depressive symptoms from bereavement may need to be quite different from treating depressive symptoms from other causes.

While medications may cause some symptoms of anxiety and depression, we hear over and over from those taking tranquilizers and antidepressants that their symptoms persist or, in some cases, are worse. With the many feelings associated with grief, "The only way through it is through it." Medication doesn't make the pain of grief go away. People need to understand this important point.

Most people expect to feel better after the first year following a loss, and they become frightened when they instead feel worse as they approach the second year. For anyone grieving a significant loss and especially for someone who has lost a spouse or life partner, the first year is a time of learning to adjust and physically survive.

Love endures death. The loss of a significant loved one is something that is not gotten "over." Words like "closure" may evoke anger and hostility on the part of the bereaved. Things (doors, lids, bank accounts) are closed. How, then, does closure apply to a relationship that is, was and always will be significant? The work of grief involves learning to live with and adjust to the loss. There may be a sense that you are never finished with grief, but realistic goals of grief work include regaining an interest in life and feeling hopeful again.

# Grieving the Loss
# of a Sibling

# My Big Sis – Gloria Steele Vaughn

My sister Gloria died on May 8, 2008

This beautiful lady was my mentor, and she taught me all about how to live an abundant life. Your life may not always be the way you want it, but you can live a joyful and rewarding life. Gloria was my big sister, the oldest of Mom's daughters. She was so beautiful and so caring that she would call me mostly on the weekends to "check up on me." Not that she was my Mom, she was my Big Sister, and Mom had raised us all to look after each other. She would ask me all about my new job I had started after college and what other plans I had for my life.

In 1979, I was also planning to marry Michael. I wouldn't have made it through all the wedding planning had she not been there for me. She just knew exactly how to plan and coordinate events. She was big on tradition, and she wanted my wedding to be the best day of my life! It was such a beautiful affair, and everything fell right in place. Her son, Tyrus, was my ring bearer.

Gloria was married for over forty years, and she knew what it took to have a successful marriage. She shared her experiences with me and told me that my marriage was just that, "Mine." I was not to compare my relationship to anyone else's. We are all different and how we relate inside our martial relationship was for us. What worked for me may not work for the next couple, and vice versa.

I got the call from Tyree (my brother-in-law) that Gloria had died early that morning. I was seated at my desk at work at the time, and it seemed that all my reasoning left me. I had just talked and laughed on the phone with her over the weekend. I shared with her my desire to be an author. She encouraged me each time we talked. I sent her cards and would write special messages inside. Gloria told me I had a gift God wanted to use. She loved the Lord, and our talks would always go to the study of God's Word.

Without being able to talk to Gloria, life was hard. I would pick up the phone and then realize that she was not there. I struggled to find someone like her to confide in. She was a beautiful soul God called home, and she is happy living with her God.

I will always love you Gloria, and I know you are there for me anytime I need to talk. You will forever be in my heart.

Your little Sis

# My Sweet Sister – Carolyn Covington

Carolyn died on May 12, 2012.

Lord, how do I figure out where to go to now? Carolyn and I were very close. She and I were seven years apart in age, and I was the daughter born after her. She always told me, "1 was her doll baby," and she loved taking care of me as a child. Carolyn and I loved many of the same things in life: fashion, makeup, dancing, and laughing. Carolyn was a great joke teller and always remembered the punch lines. Our childhood had hard times, yet there were good times. We learned to depend on each other as children and had each other's back in times of trouble.

Carolyn was a hard worker and had the love for all of us in her heart. Her house was the gathering place when we all grew up. We would sit on her porch and in her yard and share in the many stories of our childhood. Carolyn got sick and bore her illness like a true soldier of the Lord. She wasn't one to complain because she was "too busy living," and she didn't want anyone to feel as if they had to do anything for her.

Carolyn taught me how to live independently while still married. She remarked, "Don't lose yourself in your marriage, because you are still an individual." Wow! That was a true revelation to me. You can still have your dreams and work towards them without causing a rift in your marriage. Learn to talk through your issues and don't run from them. Greatest advice ever, Sis!

We were like two peas in a pod, and I don't think the realization of Carolyn's death truly hit me until a year after she had died. I was so busy trying to keep going and trying to look out for her son, Trent, the love of her life. She loved him with an undying love and sacrificed much for his comfort. The adjustment period was hard, but somehow I made it through.

One of the things I have from Carolyn is her Bible. I read it sometimes and feel close to her. I look at the scripture she underlined and at her writings in the margins as she studied God's Word. She could sit down and tell wonderful stories of how God had brought her through many nights. Carolyn was so strong! In her faith and in her resolve she knew God would always take care of her. She never doubted his love for her nor the way she had to go through her illnesses. She always remembered that He loved her.

I love you, too, Carolyn. Thank you for all you taught me, forever in my heart, Sis.

# My Big Brother – James William Steele

My brother died on April 10, 1991.

My Big Brother James was a sweet loving and kind soul. James loved people, and they loved him. He was born a Leo, and he was a strong lion who protected his siblings. He wouldn't allow anything to harm us. James was our father figure when our father and mother separated. He never complained and just stepped up to the plate and did his job. He took on the responsibility of being a great listener, hearing our problems and helping with reminders for class activities and worrying when we had doctors appointments.

James was a worker in the Surgical Department at Baptist Hospital for over twenty-five years. He loved his job and the people he served. James attended school for awhile then moved to Nashville to care for his grandmother. He visited us on every other Saturday. He would ride the Interurban Bus and come visit with family and friends over the weekend. Each Sunday night he would board the bus and go back to Nashville to his job at Baptist Hospital. My proudest moment was when he walked me down the aisle to marry Michael Smith.

Years went by and then one day the news came to the family that James had an illness that would eventually take his life. The family was in shock, but we held on to our faith. We were all young and hopeful, and we prayed he would get better in time. I visited him every other day. I was pregnant at the time with my third child, Quandré, and James was always teasing me and asking me what I was eating? I loved James, and I will forever miss him as  my loving brother, mentor, and friend. I couldn't have asked for a more loving and dependable person to be my brother.

James was quiet and peaceable, and he loved my mother more than anything. He was her first born child and they had a special bond. He telephoned her daily. Our mother remarked often, "I can set my watch by the time James calls me. He's always on time."

James had become gravely ill. My mother, Aunt Mattie, Gloria, and I were at the hospital when James died. He passed away knowing he was loved and appreciated for all he did for the family. We loved him deeply, and now, he is with the Lord.

# My Baby Brother –
# Michael Edward Covington

My Brother died on November 9, 2017.

Michael was the baby boy of the family. He was always treated as such and was, in fact, a little spoiled. He and I were best friends during our school years. He was always depending on me to help him with his school work. I did not mind it at all. I have always loved school and taking on a bit of extra work, was ok. He was a friendly person and had many friends. Michael, did not meet a stranger!

You could see that hand of his raised high above the crowd waving and smiling at everyone he saw. He was pleasant and concerned for the welfare of his siblings. He cherished Mama and took good care of her while she was in the Nursing Facility. He would visit her and loved to eat breakfast with her. His laughter was loud and purposeful. He had a need to be happy and he did not allow too much to bring him down.  He could always find a way to rise back up time after time.

He spent time in the U.S. Army and was a man who believed in commitment. My fondest memories are when we would sit and talk on the front porch about life. Michael's expectations were simple, to have a home, to have someone who loved him, and to help others. He led a simple life that was filled with love for whomever he met. All his neighbors loved him because he looked out for them. He would take their trash to the curb, pick up groceries for them at the store, pick up their mail. He would do small things that meant a lot to others. I can see you waving still. I can see you caring for the ones you loved. I can see you as you were the last to fill the family plot. I know you are no longer alive here on this earth, but Michael I see you alive and well in my heart.

Because of your suicide I've had to learn another way to survive your death. I do not blame you because the pain was too great for you to bear. You just wanted the pain to stop and must have felt this was your only way out. I will never blame you nor judge you for what you did.

I love you forever, and I will always be your little Sis.

# My Quiet Brother –
# Larry Morris Covington

My brother died on August 14, 2011.

Larry was the quiet brother. He was the brother who loved to cook, read, and travel. He wanted things to be different for himself and not live in Franklin all his life. He made friends easily and was very good at helping others in their time of need.

He was a good painter, landscaper, and loved working with his hands. He did not care much for fighting or arguments and was particular about his dress. He was so caring of Mama and he could be found just about every other summer repainting her porch furniture, cleaning the windows, and waxing the kitchen floors. Larry and I went fishing on the Harpeth River with friends and he had to show off just how good he was at fishing. I always wanted to be around the "guys" because they seemed to have more fun. I soon realized they got into more trouble, therefore, getting "more spankings." I soon learned to stop following them as much.

I remember when Larry left home to move to Florida and then to West Virginia and finally to Dallas. He was always moving to get a better job or to enjoy a better lifestyle. When he died in Dallas, I had the responsibility of bringing him home for burial. My brother Robert and I worked together to fulfill his dying wish. He is now resting alongside his brother Michael, James, and our Mother.

God rest your soul, sweet brother of mine. Until we meet again in heaven.  Much love.

# Grieving the Loss
# of a Parent

# My Mother – Bertha C. Covington

Mama went home to be with the Lord on September 15, 2014.

To lose her was devasting and so overwhelming all at once! My Mama was one of the most devoted mothers, hard-working women, full of the Gospel, and such a wonderful person to have known. Mama believed in teaching us the life lessons so they would stay with us for life. She was a true disciplinarian, and she taught us that bad behavior would not be rewarded. Mama was full of life. She loved to cook, clean and take care of all ten of her children. She married Daddy when she was eighteen and starting taking care of him. A young family soon ensued.

I loved to hear Mama tell the stories of her childhood. She was born and raised in the country hillside of Williamson County, Tennessee, in Thompson Station. She loved the country living. Mama taught us that times could be hard, but it was how you prepared yourself for your future that granted you a better life. She was educated in the Williamson County rural school system. She attended the Goose Creek School that was located on Goose Creek Bypass and at that time they lived on Henpeck Lane. She watched her parents work and farm the land. They attended Connection Hill Primitive Baptist Church, where her mother, Sister Lina Steele Beasley, was an usher. Life was hard but the joy came in serving the Lord. Mama learned at an early age that serving the Lord would payoff after awhile. She had one older sister, Mattie Steele Thompson Simmons, and one brother, Sam Henry Steele, Jr. Mama was the middle child, and she looked up to her older sister and cherished her younger brother.

I live my life today based on all my mother taught me. She was a great teacher, allowed us to make our mistakes and told us to learn from them. Education was a big thing for her, and she declared, "If you don't get an education, it will be your own fault because the door is open. Just go in." Mama had many wise expressions, and we loved and still use many of them today. Mama's laughter was so sweet that it filled the house like the wonderful smells of her cooking. She took great pride in all she did. Mama didn't take on the responsibility of doing anything unless she knew it would be the best she could do – another one of those nuggets she passed on to her children.

Mama gave us the greatest gift we could ever receive when she took us to the little old wood-framed church called that "Holiness Church." The church was pastored by Bishop H.C. Nesbitt. There we were taught of the love of Jesus and how He can save our soul, and if we would allow the Holy Ghost to come and dwell in our hearts, our lives would be made better. Each of Mama's children obeyed her, and we all learned well of the beauty of Holiness. Mama was baptized in Jesus on January 1, 1969, in the Green Street Church of God. What a glorious day for her, and she led us to be baptized, too.

When Mama died, I knew where her soul immediately went. She talked of heaven and all it's glory. She said one day she would live there with Jesus forever. She would walk the streets of gold and visit with family, again. I know you are in heaven Mama, and I know Jesus is your Savior and King. She often commented, "Brenda, when God comes for me, I will be ready." He came for her early that September morning, and no doubt in my mind my Mama was ready to go.

Mama, sweet eternal rest to your soul. I love and thank you for all you did for me. One day I will see you again in heaven.

# Grieving the Loss
## of a Spouse

# My Husband – Michael Wade Smith

Michael was elevated to heaven on March 3, 2010.

I could not imagine being without or not talking to Michael for one day, let alone now nine years! And how I loved this man and enjoyed his company. We could talk for hours about nothing at all. He was one of the most intelligent, brave, and sincere people I have had the pleasure of knowing. He was so loving and strong in all he did for me and his family. Aaah, the love he had for us was unmatched by anything in the world. We were first, and he considered it a pleasure to take care of us. He was a wonderful and sacrificial provider for me and his children. He gave us his all.

I had the pleasure of meeting Michael at Nashville Tech in Nashville after I graduated high school. I was on the technical administrative track in school, so I applied to Nashville Tech and was accepted and started in the Fall of 1975. I was working in the library and saw him studying. He had books all around him, like a mountain. He had this huge afro, the sweetest smile and the most gorgeous brown eyes I had ever seen! He was courteous and soft-spoken with an encouraging word to all his friends at Tech. I learned later he was studying to be an Electronics Engineer. He rode a motorcycle and loved playing ping-pong. (He was really good at it, even though he was left handed.) He made friends easily, and everyone loved to just sit and talk with him. He seemed to have an answer to everything, and if he didn't know the answer, he knew where to tell you to find it. The library was his haven!

Michael and I became an item on campus. We dated for three years, our remaining time at Tech. After Tech he joined the United

States Air Force in April of 1979. We married in December 1979, and I joined him in April 1980. We made a beautiful life together in Cheyenne, Wyoming, for three years. When he separated out of the service in 1983, we made Nashville, then Franklin our permanent home. God blessed us with three beautiful children and thirty years of marriage. Michael loved life and was a great father and husband. He worked long hours and was a constant learner, who thought education was supreme in your life. All of our children exceled in higher education. I returned to college in 2010 and received my Bachelor's degree.

Michael's love for us will forever be in our hearts and in our minds. We will never ever forget the love, tenderness, and sacrifice he made for me and his family. We cherish each memory and will always hold him dear to our hearts. He was a great Sergeant in the U.S. Air Force and is buried in the field of honor where he will always be with his comrades from all the Armed Forces.

Michael, there isn't a day that goes by that I don't think of you and love you. I learned that love never dies. I know you are with each of us daily, and we feel your spirit within us. I will never get over losing you, but with God's help I have learned to get past it. This book is for you and to help others know that as hard as it is to lose that special love of your life – God keeps them safe in His arms.

Always and forever my love for you will be true. Until we meet again in heaven, rest well my love.

# Life After Death

**Life After Death – why is it such a hot topic?**

Life after death – Why all the interest? Combine events like September 11th with the demographic phenomenon of the Baby Boomer generation reaching its 60s, and suddenly the reality of death from catastrophe and death from mere old age are upon us in a personal way.

It appears that more and more people are asking the same question that Job asked nearly 4,000 years ago in the Bible, "If a man dies, will he live again?" What could be a more fundamental question of life and death? Reincarnation theories are popular in Eastern religions as well as the many New Age variants. It seems people are comfortable with the idea of another chance to return to earth and figure things out or make things right. Some nihilist thinkers believe death is the absolute end; but contrary to what many might think, most people believe that death is not the end. In some shape or form, we go on.

When Jesus was talking with Martha about the death of Lazarus, her brother, He declared, "I am the Resurrection and the life. He who believes in me will live, even though he dies; and whoever lives and believes in me will never die." Right here, Jesus presents the astonishing claim there's life after death. Jesus then took the next step and brought Lazarus back to life after four days in a tomb. At that point, Jesus put everyone on notice that He would later overcome the grave Himself!

*"For God so loved the world that He gave His one and only Son, that whoever believes in Him shall not perish, but have eternal life."*

John 3:16

For skeptics, the whole idea of heaven is just the product of fertile imaginations. For many others, the biblical idea of heaven is too fanciful or fantastic. However, Christians can live their lives with bold hope, thanks to the evidence of history that establishes with convincing clarity how Jesus not only preceded us in death, but also came back from the dead and blazed the trail to heaven.

**Life After Death – Proof?**

Is there mathematical proof for life after death? No. But if you believe the life-changing evidence for God, Jesus and the Bible, then heaven is as much a concrete reality for you as the Lord in whom you've invested your absolute trust. It's not fantasy; it's the absolute life-changing hope that strengthens us and gives us peace.

*"] write these things to you who believe in the name of the Son of God, so that you may know that you have eternal life.* "

1 John 5:12

**Will we recognize and be reunited with our loved ones in heaven?**

Yes! In the Old Testament, when a person died, the biblical writers said he was "gathered to his people" (Gen. 25:8, 35:29, 49:29; Num. 20:24; Judges 2:10). In 2 Sainuel 12, when David's infant child died, David confidently announced, "I shall go to him, but he shall not return to me" (v. 23). David evidently expected to see the child again – not just a nameless, faceless soul without an identity, but that very child.

The New Testament indicates even more clearly that our identities will remain unchanged. While sharing the Passover meal with His disciples, Christ spoke, "Take this [cup] and divide it among yourselves; for I say to you, I will not drink of the fruit of the vine until the kingdom of God comes." (Luke 22:17-18) Christ was promising that He and His disciples would drink the fruit of the vine together again in heaven. Elsewhere, Jesus makes a similar, but even more definite, promise, "Many will come from east and west, and sit down with Abraham, Isaac, and Jacob in the kingdom of heaven." (Matt. 8:11)

Furthermore, Moses and Elijah appeared with Christ on the Mount of Transfiguration. Even though it had been centuries since Moses died and Elijah was taken to heaven, they still maintained a clear identity (Matt. 17:3). Peter, James and John evidently recognized them (v. 4), which implies that we will somehow be able to recognize people we've never seen before.

All the redeemed will maintain their identity forever, but in a perfected form. We will be able to have fellowship with Enoch, Noah, Abraham, Jacob, Samuel, Moses, Joshua, Esther, Elijah, Elisha, Isaiah, Daniel, Ezekiel, David, Peter, Barnabas, Paul, or any of the saints we choose. For that to be possible, we must all retain our individual identities, not turn into some sort of generic beings.

Describing the Lord's appearing and the resurrection of the saints who have died, Paul writes, "Then we who are alive and remain shall be caught up together with them in the clouds to meet the Lord in the air. And thus we shall always be with the Lord." (1 Thess. 4:17)

Paul's purpose in writing was to comfort some of the Thessalonians who evidently thought their dying loved ones would miss the return of Christ. He says in verse 18, "Comfort one another with these words." The comfort comes from the prospect of reunion. Little comfort this would be if in the reunion we could not even recognize one another. But Paul's promise that we will all be "together" forever implies that we shall renew fellowship with all whom we have known.

We will be reunited not only with our own families and loved ones, but also with the people of God from all ages. In heaven we will all be one loving family. The immense size of the family will not matter in the infinite perfection of heaven. There will be ample opportunity for close relationships with everyone, and our eternity will be spent in just that kind of rich, unending fellowship.

If you're worried about feeling out of place in heaven, don't Heaven will seem more like home than the dearest spot on earth to you. It is uniquely designed by a tender, loving Savior to be the place where we will live together for all eternity and enjoy Him forever in the fullness of our glorified humanity.

Is it any wonder that the psalmist said, "Precious in the sight of the Lord is the death of His saints." (Psalm 116:15)

# Eight Keys to Remember When the Body of a Beloved Soul Dies

**1. Remember that you will see them again, and can now.** Much clinical data from near-death experiences, life between life sessions, and evidential mediums indicate when you pass on, you enjoy a glorious reunion with loved ones who graduated from earth school before you. What's more, you don't have to wait until you pass on to experience the real presence of your dear family, friends, and pets.

Many people have experienced after-death contacts while awake or dreaming, via the usual senses or more ethereal ones. How can you get bigger eyes? Pray you will sense your loved ones' presence; meditate to become quiet and peaceful so you can perceive their subtle presence; walk in nature and talk to them as though they are right there, because they are.

**2. Celebrate, since they graduated from earth school:** many cultures throw a party when a loved one physical dies. Why? Because they know she has completed her lessons. They also know about #1 so they can accept that life is never-ending, but periodically changing. You can do the same.

This knowledge allows you to experience sadness and pain, and at the same time, feel joy that they are enjoying the next stage of forever. It's similar to the bitter-sweet feelings when young people graduate from high school: you're happy they finished, but sad they will be leaving home.

**3. Know that they are having a wonderful experience:** unless your departed loved one was named Hitler or another apparently dastardly villain, she is having a great time. Here's one way to gauge how wonderful your loved ones are feeling in the next realm. Recall your very best days while on earth: your happiest, healthiest, and most energetic. Then multiply that by a million. That's how good it feels to return to the Light, or more accurately, remember you are an integral part of it now and forever.

'When your bodily limbs have died, then shall you truly dance.'

Does #3 sound too good to be true? Sometimes life on earth involves so many disappointments and struggles that it's hard to believe in good news. That's why it's important to know the evidence that each of us can enjoy a heavenly afterlife.

Breathe deeply again as you remember – for your essence knows this very well – that physical death is a portal to higher energy realms.

Imagine how awful your feet would feel after walking all day in a pair of ill-fitting shoes. Now consider how wonderful it would feel to slip them off and soak your feet in a tub of warm water. That is fraction of how good it feels to drop your body – especially when it is aged or chronically ill and tired. And that's what your loved ones who have crossed over are feeling.

**4. Make your life a work of ART:** A.RT. is an acronym for *Appreciate, Realize,* and *Transform.* When a loved one's physical body dies, you can consciously choose to:

> • Appreciate the time you spent together and the wonderful memories that are accessible throughout eternity. You also can focus on gratitude that she is now joyful, peaceful, whole, and free of earth's difficulties.

> • Realize you will see him again when you pass on and can likely learn to sense his very real presence now.

> • Transform yourself for the better to honor and create more meaning to his life. This also helps you grow, evolve, and serve others from a higher level.

Each time you start to feel sad, lonely, and discouraged, remind yourself that you can shift your focus.

Please take a moment right now to think about a difficult event in your life and how you can apply the A.R.T. formula. Doing this will create the habit of focusing on more positive emotions. You will then be prepared when the next big change or challenge occurs.

Take another deep breath to center and remember. Rachel wrote me about the time since her son graduated from this phase of life into the next: "The past eleven months have been a time of the greatest pain, yet also the most growth I have ever experienced." What an amazing statement. And that is how it can be for everyone. Rachel is now helping others with her mediumistic skills that burgeoned after her son's passing. And he is helping her from another dimension.

**5. Know what your loved ones are trying to tell you.** You can visit a highly skilled evidential medium in hopes of getting specific messages from your dear ones who have changed worlds. However, some mediums are outright fakes while others are very mediocre. The really great ones are very busy.

You can save a lot of time and money since those in spirit share very similar messages. They want you to:

- be happy and peaceful now
- know they are very much alive and well
- not worry about them
- fully enjoy your remaining time on earth
- know you will see each other again
- release guilt and self-blame for anything you did or didn't do while they were on earth

**6. Realize that death is an important part of life:** We all have wondered, "Why do we have to die? Why can't everyone just live forever?" The answer is simple: we don't really die; we just change outward form. To those who only view life with the five senses, the change looks like a scary end of existence.

Also, imagine how boring and stifling a constant sameness would be. Here's one way to do this: think of your favorite movie and ask yourself, "Would you want to watch it all day and every day for eternity?" Of course not. Well, it's very much the same way with life. Souls love variety, expansion, challenge, and adventure, not safe stagnation. Life is designed to include perpetual change. It's a great setup when you release fear. Remember you are an eternal being, and realize there's meaning to it all.

Have you ever found yourself wishing you could freeze time and things would never change? It's a natural thought, especially if everything seems optimal for you. But a little contemplation about this will help you realize how bad of a plan that would be. If you need more proof, watch the movie Groundhog Day over and over.

**7. Use and share their gifts:** Various cultures believe loved ones can send a spiritual gift to you after they graduate from earth school. Some people on earth have noticed a marked change in their personality or energy after a dear one passes on. Perhaps, they received an energetic gift from those who moved on to higher energy realms.

You are an energetic being living in an energy universe. Your interactions result in a literal exchange of physical molecules and energies – particles and waves. Just imagine the transfer of love, ideas, and inspiration that can occur when your loved ones change worlds. You can use their gifts to lighten your grief, heal and transform yourself and the world.

**8. Lean on others.** Just as the classic song, "Lean On Me," by Bill Withers encourages, we need to lean on each other at times. Even though they are in extreme pain and grief, some people feel they don't want to bother others. You'll be surprised by how many people are glad and honored to help. When you get back on your feet, you can pay it forward and assist someone else. It's a simple but elegant model for following the Golden Rule and enjoying a wonderful life here and now.

# What Does the Bible Say About Overcoming Grief?

Grief is an emotion common to the human experience, and we witness the process of grief throughout the biblical narrative. Multiple Bible characters experienced deep loss and sadness, including Job, Naomi, Hannah, and David. Even Jesus mourned (John 11:35, Matthew 23:37–39). After Lazarus died, Jesus went to the village of Bethany, where Lazarus was buried. When Jesus saw Martha and the other mourners weeping, He also wept. He was moved by their grief and also by the fact of Lazarus's death. The astounding thing is that, even though Jesus knew He was going to raise Lazarus from the dead, He chose to partake of the grief of the situation. Jesus truly is a high priest who can "sympathize with our weaknesses." (Hebrews 4:15)

One step in overcoming grief is having the right perspective on it. First, we recognize that grief is a natural response to pain and loss. There is nothing wrong with grieving. Second, we know that times of grief serve a purpose. Ecclesiastes 7:2 says, "It is better to go to the house of mourning than to go to the house of feasting, for this is the end of all mankind, and the living will lay it to heart." This verse implies that grief can be good because it can refresh our perspective on life. Third, we remember that feelings of grief are temporary. "Weeping may remain for a night, but rejoicing comes in the morning." (Psalm 30:5) There is an end to mourning. Grief has its purpose, but it also has its limit.

Through it all, God is faithful. There are many scriptures that remind us of God's faithfulness in times of mourning. He is with us even in the valley of the shadow of death (Psalm 23:4). When

David sorrowed, he prayed this in Psalm 56:8: "You have kept count of my tossings; put my tears in your bottle. Are they not in your book?" The touching image of God catching our tears is full of meaning. He sees our grief and does not disdain it. Like Jesus entered into the grief of the mourners in Bethany, God enters into our grief. At the same time, He reassures us that all is not lost. Psalm 46:10 reminds us to "be still" and rest in the knowledge that He is God. He is our refuge (Psalm 91:1–2). He works all things together for the good of those He has called (Romans 8:28).

An important part of overcoming grief is expressing it to God. The Psalms contain numerous examples of pouring out one's heart to God. Interestingly, the psalmist never ends where he began. He may start a psalm with expressions of grief, but almost invariably, he will end it with praise (Psalm 13, Psalm 23:4, Psalm 30:11–12, Psalm 56). God understands us (Psalm 139:2). When we commune with Him, we are able to open our minds to the truth that He loves us, that He is faithful, that He is in control, and that He knows how He is going to work it out for our good.

Another important step in overcoming grief is to share it with others. The body of Christ is designed to ease the burdens of its individual members (Galatians 6:2), and fellow believers have the ability to "mourn with those who mourn" (Romans 12:15). Often, the grieving tend to shun others, increasing feelings of isolation and misery. It is much healthier to seek counseling, and group settings can be invaluable. Groups offer listening ears and helpful encouragement, camaraderie, and guidance in working through the grief. When we share our stories with God and others, our grief is lessened.

Sadly, grief is part of the human experience. Loss is part of life, and grief is a natural response to loss. But we have the hope of Christ, and we know that He is strong enough to carry our burdens (Matthew 11:30). We can give our hurt to Him because He cares for us (1 Peter 5:7). We can find solace in the Holy Spirit, our Comforter and Paraclete (John 14:16). In grief, we cast our burdens on Him, rely on the community of the church and delve into the truth of the Word.

# Bible Verses for Overcoming Grief

God has a "word" for everything, every situation and every circumstance that arises in your life. Grieving can be the most difficult time for people. Trying to balance the feelings of pain and loss while going forward with your life, can be difficult. With this collection of Bible verses, we can turn to God with the confidence that His Word will help us to ease and comfort as we overcome grief.

*He will wipe every tear from their eyes. There will be no more death or mourning or crying or pain, for the old order of things has passed away.*
Revelation 21:4

*The Lord is close to the brokenhearted and saves those who are crushed in spirit.*
Psalm 34:18

*He heals the brokenhearted and binds up their wounds.*
Psalm 147:3

*Now when Jesus saw the crowds, he went up on a mountainside and sat down. His disciples came to him, and he began to teach them. He said: "Blessed are they who mourn for they shall be comforted."*
Matthew 51:3

*My flesh and my heart may fail, but God is the strength of my heart and my portion forever.*
Psalm 73:26

*Do not let you heart be troubled, You believe in God; believe also in me.*
John 14:1

*Surely he took up our pain and bore our suffering, yet we considered him punished by God, stricken by him, and afflicted. 5 But he was wounded for our transgressions, he was bruised for our iniquities; the chaistisement of our peace was upon him, and by his stripes we are healed.*

Isaiah 53:4-5


*Have I not commanded you? Be strong and courageous. Do not be afraid; do not be discouraged, for the Lord your God will be with you wherever you go.*

Joshua 1:9


*And we know that in all things God works for the good of those who love him, who have been called according to his purpose.*

Romans 8:28


*Yea, though I walk through the valley of the shadow of death, I will fear no evil; For You are with me; Your rod and Your staff, they comfort me.*

Psalm 23:4


*Praise be to the God and Father of our Lord Jesus Christ, the Father of compassion and the God of all comfort, 4 who comforts us in all our troubles, so that we can comfort those in any trouble with the comfort we ourselves receive from God.*

2 Cornithians 1:3-4


*For whatever things were written before were written for our learning, that we through the patience and comfort of the Scriptures might have hope.*

Romans 15:4


*There is a time for everything, and a season for every activity under heaven: 2 A time to be born and a time to die, a time to plant and a time to uproot. 3 A time to kill, and a time to heal; a time to break down, and a time to build up; 4 A time to weep, and a time to laugh; a time to mourn, and a time to dance.*

Ecclesiastes 3:1-4

*"Come to me, all you who are weary and burdened, and I will give you rest. 29 Take my yoke upon you and learn from me, for I am gently and humble in heart and you will find rest for your souls. 30 For my yoke is easy and my burden light."*

Matthew 11:28-30

*"When you pass through the waters, I will be with you; and when you pass through the rivers, they will not sweep over you. When you walk through the fire, you will not be burned; the flames will not set you ablaze."*

Isaiah 43:2

*We are afflicted in every way, but not crushed; perplexed, but not despairing.*

2 Corninthians 4:8

*Therefore we do not lose heart. Though outwardly we are wasting away, yet inwardly we are being renewed day by day. 17 For our light and momentary troubles are achieving for us an eternal glory that far outweighs them all. 18 So we fix our eyes not on what is seen, but on what is unseen. For what is seen is temporary, but what is unseen is eternal.*

2 Cornithians 4:16:18

*For I know the plans I have for you declares the Lord, plans to prosper you and not to harm you, plans to give you a hope and a future.*

Jeremiah 29:11

*In you, oh Lord, I have taken refuge; let me never be put to shame; deliver me in your righteousness. 2 Turn your ear to me, come quickly to my rescue; be my rock of refuge, a strong fortress to save me.*

Psalm 31:1-2

*I consider that our present sufferings are not worth comparing with the glory that will be revealed in us.*

Romans 8:18

*Brothers and sisters, we do not want you to be uninformed about those who sleep in death, so that you do not grieve like the rest of mankind, who have no hope. 14 For we believe that Jesus died and rose again, and so we believe that God will bring Jesus those who have fallen asleep in him. 15 According to the Lord's word, we tell you that we who are still alive, who are left until the coming of the Lord, will certainly not precede those who have fallen asleep. 16 For the Lord himself will come down from heaven, with a loud command, with the voice of the archangel and with the trumpet call of God, and the dead in Christ will rise first. 17 After that, we who are still alive and are left will be caught up together with them in the clouds to meet the Lord in the air. And so we will be with the Lord forever. 18 Therefore encourage one another with these words.*

I Thessalonians 4:13-18

# Grief Counseling?

What is someone looking for when they consult a counselor? Answers? Of course. Understanding and wisdom? Always. Healing? I We all need to be healed of our wounds. But what kind of approach best facilitates these things actually happening in a counseling context?

It is my belief the primary agent of healing in therapy is less about the training or theoretical orientation of the counselor and more about the cultivation of a safe, open, caring, and personal relationship in which to share your pain. When this is established, we are in a position where the healing begins. We can impart wisdom, truth, and caring directly to the person in need. I have found that when a person is hurting and in this intense pain, they are not looking for a teacher, preacher, doctor, or instructor. They are looking for a friend – a person whom they can be open and honest with. They need to talk, and they need someone who will listen.

In my journey as a survivor of these deaths, I have trusted literature, philosophy, theology, and the ongoing examination of my own life as I have had counseling myself. There are many roads to travel in seeking counseling for yourself or for someone else you know is hurting. You can select one-on-one with a counselor. You can do group counseling sessions. You can read inspirational books, and blogs. You can read the Word of God.

Your first reaction to loss, whether a death or the end of a relationship, is typically shock and disbelief. This naturally places you in a mode of denial as a person tries to avoid dealing with or recognizing the reality of the loss. In the case of a relationship, an individual may attempt to salvage the relationship or look desperately for answers as to why it failed.

Anger usually follows the denial and disbelief phase. A person may ask why the event has happened or believe it to be unfair. Bargaining can be added to this, especially in terms of prayer. The guilt stage follows as the person begins to self-blame for what happened. This is a way for people to gain mental control over a situation that appears uncontrollable.

The second-to-last stage is depression, and this is often the longest stage for many people. The final stage is accepting the loss and moving on. Often coupled with acceptance is a renewed sense of hope that things will get better, and that life does go on.

# What Grief Teaches Us

Grief is a reality we all must confront at some point. The experience of grief is different for everyone, and it has no timetable. Grieving, however, is a necessary part of the coping and healing processes.

**Live Your Best Life Now.**

Living your best life means you are going to stay focused and engaged in the reality of your life. We all must face disappointments in life, but we are still blessed with life, so we have to pick ourselves up and dust ourselves off and continue on in LIFE.

Find encouragement from people who have gone through struggles. I love this from Pastor Joel Osteen, having lost his father, he gives this as encouragement in Living Your Best Life, "God knows your value; He sees your potential. You may not understand everything you are going through right now. But hold your head up high, knowing that God is in control and he has a great plan and purpose for your life. Your dreams may not have turned out exactly as you'd hoped, but the bible says that God's ways are better and higher than our ways, even when everybody else rejects you, remember, God stands before you with His arms open wide. He always accepts you. He always confirms your value. God sees your two good moves! You are His prized possession. No matter what you go through in life, no matter how many disappointments you suffer, your value in God's eyes always remains the same. You will always be the apple of His eye. He will never give up on you, so don't give up on yourself."

## Family and Friends.

Do not turn down the offer of friends and family to help you get past your grief. Do not avoid, nor block them out of your life. When they are offering tangible help that is needed, please accept it. People truly do the best they can with the knowledge they have been given. Some may not have experienced death on the level to which you have, nor lost the loved one you have, but try to be patient with family and your friends.

## Healing is a Process – Don't Rush It

Patience is one of the best methods you will use throughout your healing process. Patient with Yourself! Don't try to rush past these emotions and try to show the world, you are healing and your wounds are still in need of attention. Take the time you need to get back on your feet and become emotional stable. Reach out and seek help when needed. Don't be ashamed that you need someone to talk to. Processes take time, and they must not be rushed in order to receive the best results.

## Use Your Power of Choice

Choose to be hopeful. Never ever give up Hope! "Hope is the thing with feathers that perches in the soul, and sings the tunes without the words, and never stops at all." – Emily Dickinson. What is life without hope? Nothing. Therefore, we have to hope in order to keep on living. "Out of the depths I cry to you, O Lord! O Lord, hear my voice! Let your ears be attentive to the voice of my pleas for mercy!" (Psalm 130:1–2) In Christ, God has paved the way for those lost in darkness to have access to him once again. And not only access, but rich fellowship! The Christian whose heart has been made new sees his or her need for hope in Christ. The Christian hopes in the assured presence of God who hears when they call, knowing that the power to overcome has been se-cured by Christ's blood. God's continual presence is a living stream that pours into the life of the believer (Psalm 1). This gives us hope because we are never alone. Jesus said he would never leave us nor forsake us.

For some people, purpose is connected to vocation – meaningful, satisfying work. For others, their purpose lies in their responsibilities to their family or friends. Others seek meaning through spirituality or religious beliefs. Some people may find their purpose clearly expressed in all these aspects of life. While each grief process is unique, the loss of someone with whom you have shared a deep emotional and supportive relationship usually causes the most intense grief reaction. Someone who has held you up emotionally when you were in crisis, helped shape your sense of self, and/or encouraged you to reach for your dreams is physically removed from your life forever. So, it makes sense that in the acute phase of grief, you may feel as though you have lost your sense of self or feel unsure of your life purpose.

Grief is an expression of love that continues after death. You shouldn't expect your grief to ever end completely. However, it is possible for your grief to become more integrated; painful emotions occur less frequently and with less intensity and no longer interfere significantly with work, other relationships, or your experience of positive emotions.

When it is time to start again, you will know. Your heart will want to reach out to help others, and you will feel an assurance that your healing has taken place. The best way to get over the loss of losing someone is to find a greater purpose in helping others.

### Don't Run Away From Life: Stay Strong and Embrace Its Unpredictability

For those of us left behind, it's important we ask ourselves what our loved ones would want for us after they die. Would they want us drowning in the grief and despair of their loss, or would they want us to mourn, make peace with and move past their deaths? We also need to remember our time here is limited. We need to stop putting off until tomorrow, those things that will add value and meaning to our lives today. Don't let fear of failure, success or judgment by others keep you from realizing your full potential. Give yourself permission to be all that you can be and unapologetically move in the direction of your dreams.

# Goodbye Letter

To_____

I need to say goodbye because_____

_____

_____

My most cherished memory of you is_____

_____

_____

_____

_____

You taught me_____

_____

_____

_____

I always wanted to tell you_____

_____

_____

_____

I will always remember you because_____

_____

_____

_____

From_____

# About Brenda Smith

When meeting Brenda C. Smith, for the first time, you will soon discover this overjoyed, full of life Christian woman "walks her talk."

"I've always loved to write. I started writing poetry at a very early age, and thought it was great the way I could make the words rhyme. I was hooked! Not only on the rhyming of the words, but having the ability to put in words what beauty I saw in nature and the experiences in my life," exclaims Brenda. Her mother encouraged her to write – pursuing the thing that makes you happy was your gift in life.

Brenda loves the Word of God and how it makes her feel loved, wanted and needed in this world. She grew up attending church back in the times when you went to church at 10:00 a.m. on a Sunday morning, and you came back home after the 6:00 p.m. night service. "We 'churched' all day, and I wouldn't have it any other way," remarks Brenda. Without the Gospel of Jesus Christ, Brenda whole-heartily believes that we would all be lost, and it is her duty as a Christian to help lift the spirit of those who are down-trodden.

After attending her first writer's workshop, Brenda left with the determination someday she would be a writer of Christian literature. Now, she writes articles for several Christian publications. "My

God, my family and my work have provided a vast array of subject matter for my writing," remarks Brenda. She also conducts a ministry called B.A.L.M. (Bereavement and Loss Ministry), helping others through the grieving process. Brenda's "Thursday's Word" blog is emailed weekly as an outreach to encourage people who are having struggles in life. Her first book, *Thursday's Word*, is a collection of biblical devotionals and poetry from her popular weekly blog. As you absorb Brenda Smith's devotionals and poetry, she will inspire you to "Walk Your Talk" in your daily Christian life.

Brenda attended Lipscomb University in Nashville, Tennessee, majoring in Business Administration and Biblical Ethics. She was awarded a Bachelor of Religious Education degree from Tennessee Bible College, Cookeville, Tennessee.

Brenda has three children: Quinton, Quinesha, and Quandre' and one grandson, Caneen, who is her "joy." Brenda resides in historic Franklin, Tennessee.

# ORDER COPIES OF THIS BOOK NOW!

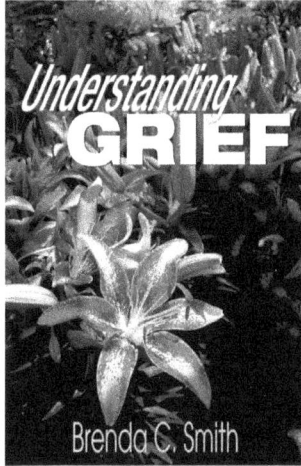

NO. OF COPIES___*Understanding Grief* @ $11$^{.95}$ each ___x no. of copies

| | |
|---|---|
| SUBTOTAL | _____ |
| Add 9.25 % sales tax (Tenn.. residents only) | _____ |
| Postage and handling for 1st book - $3$^{.75}$ | _____ |
| P & H for each additional book - $1$^{.00}$ | _____ |
| TOTAL | _____ |

ORDERED BY _____

STREET/APT NO. _____

CITY/STATE/ZIP_____

PHONE (_____)_____

Your email address: _____
We would like to send you product updates by email.

MAKE YOUR CHECK OR MONEY ORDER TO: BRENDA C. SMITH
**PLEASE MAIL THIS ORDER FORM WITH YOUR PAYMENT TO:**
Brenda C. Smith, P.O. Box 405, Franklin TN 37064
Please allow 2 weeks for delivery. Prices are subject to change without notice.

# ORDER COPIES OF THIS BOOK NOW!

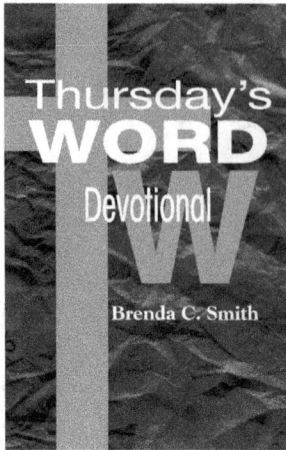

NO. OF COPIES___Thursday's Word @ $17$^{.95}$ each ___x no. of copies

| | |
|---|---|
| SUBTOTAL | _____ |
| Add 9.25 % sales tax (Tenn. residents only) | _____ |
| Postage and handling for 1st book - $3$^{.75}$ | _____ |
| P & H for each additional book - $1$^{.00}$ | _____ |
| TOTAL | _____ |

ORDERED BY _____

STREET/APT NO. _____

CITY/STATE/ZIP_____

PHONE (_____)_____

Your email address: _____
We would like to send you product updates by email.

MAKE YOUR CHECK OR MONEY ORDER TO: BRENDA C. SMITH
**PLEASE MAIL THIS ORDER FORM WITH YOUR PAYMENT TO:**
Brenda C. Smith, P.O. Box 405, Franklin TN 37064
Please allow 2 weeks for delivery. Prices are subject to change without notice.

**incahoots LITERARY** presents our latest books

*Just A Cowboy* — Kenny Phipps

*HUNTER* — W. Neil Gallagher

*His Word in Troubled Times* — Janice Brown

*The Man-eater of Mfuwe* — Wayne Hosek

*Never Marry a Boyt Man*

*Can a Sperm Swim Backwards?* — Susan Hunger

*SUNDAY CREEK* — Jeff Cheresky

*My Sermon Notes* — Bishop Kenneth O. Robinson

*My Sermon Notes Volume 2* — Bishop Kenneth O. Robinson

*Tales B-O Ranch* — Buck

*The Cost of Innocence* — Debbra Macdonald

*the Right to Fit* — Kimberly Kuykendall

*OPERATION PayBack* — Maria M. Stephens

*RUSTY and the CIRCUS OF DOUBT* — O. Russell Reynolds

*Celebration* — Patti Jo Hogan-Hostetler

*Sonshine Devotionals* — Jeanette Elrod

*Thursday's WORD Devotional* — Brenda C. Smith

*Legend in my Spare Mind*

*My Sermon Notes Volume 3* — Bishop Kenneth O. Robinson

*Understanding GRIEF* — Brenda C. Smith

For book information
and to order your
InCahoots Literary books
*Visit*
*incahootsliterary.com*

# Everyone has a story to tell.

## Have you written a book?

### InCahoots Literary
#### could be your
### PUBLISHER

We take your manuscript, put it in book form and place your new book in the marketplace. We can also develop your promotional and marketing strategies. We love authors who will promote and sell their books in every possible way.

For more information, visit our Web site:
## www.incahootsliterary.com

inCahoots
LITERARY

www.ingramcontent.com/pod-product-compliance
Lightning Source LLC
Chambersburg PA
CBHW050558280326
41933CB00011B/1900